Stars and Galaxies

Secrets of the Universe

Giles Sparrow

WORLD ALMANAC® LIBRARY

Please visit our web site at: www.garethstevens.com
For a free color catalog describing World Almanac® Library's list of high-quality books
and multimedia programs, call 1-800-848-2928 (USA) or 1-800-387-3178 (Canada).
World Almanac® Library's fax: (414) 332-3567.

Library of Congress Cataloging-in-Publication Data

Sparrow, Giles.
    Stars and galaxies / by Giles Sparrow.
      p. cm. — (Secrets of the universe)
    Includes bibliographical references and index.
    ISBN-10: 0-8368-7280-0 — ISBN-13: 978-0-8368-7280-4 (lib. bdg.)
    ISBN-10: 0-8368-7287-8 — ISBN-13: 978- 0-8368-7287-3 (softcover)
    1. Stars—Juvenile literature. 2. Galaxies—Juvenile literature. I. Title.
  II. Series: Sparrow, Giles. Secrets of the universe. III. Series.
  QB801.7.S657   2007
  523.8—dc22   2006009961

This North American edition first published in 2007 by
World Almanac® Library
A Member of the WRC Media Family of Companies
330 West Olive Street, Suite 100
Milwaukee, WI 53212 USA

This U.S. edition copyright © 2007 by World Almanac® Library. Original edition copyright
© 2006 by IMP. FProduced by Amber Books Ltd., Bradley's Close, 74–77 White Lion Street,
London N1 9PF, U.K.

Amber Books project editor: James Bennett
Amber Books design: Richard Mason
Amber Books picture research: Terry Forshaw

World Almanac® Library editor: Carol Ryback
World Almanac® Library designer: Scott M. Krall
World Almanac® Library art direction: Tammy West
World Almanac® Library production: Jessica Morris and Robert Kraus

Picture acknowledgements: All photographs courtesy of NASA except for the following:
CORBIS: 4 (Roger Ressmeyer); 19 (Bettmann). Getty Images: 23 (Hulton Archive). All artwork
courtesy of International Masters Publishers Ltd.

Printed in the United States of America

1 2 3 4 5 6 7 8 9 10 09 08 07 06

CONTENTS

LIGHTS IN THE SKY   4

THE SUN   14

LIFE STORIES   22

ANATOMY OF A GALAXY   30

A UNIVERSE OF GALAXIES   38

GLOSSARY   46

FURTHER INFORMATION   47

INDEX   48

Cover and title page: Our Milky Way galaxy, a barred spiral, roughly mimics the structure of spiral galaxy NGC 2997, shown here. Swirling dark lines mark heavy concentrations of space dust, while the bluish areas of its arms signal stellar nurseries.

Betelgeuse

Orion's Belt

Orion's Sword

Sirius

Rigel

LIGHTS IN THE SKY

L ook up on a clear dark night, and the sky seems filled with countless stars. On average, twenty-five hundred are visible to the naked eye from anywhere on Earth. They vary in brightness and color, and if you look at them through a pair of binoculars, you will see they are just the brightest of a multitude of stars. Some form close pairs, others vary in brightness from night to night or from year to year, and a few may burst suddenly into visibility before fading away again. Even the most powerful telescope, however, will not transform any of these tiny points of light into a noticeable disk—a hint of just how far away the stars actually lie.

How can we learn more about objects that are so far away we cannot even see them properly? Fortunately, astronomers have developed a range of powerful methods for finding out as much as possible from what little they can observe.

Using these techniques and some basic laws of physics, they are able to discover many of the properties of stars.

Brightness and distance

It seems obvious to state that the stars in the sky have different levels of brightness, but even this tells us a surprising amount of information. The range of brightness must mean that they are not all the same distance from us or from each other (in fact, both statements are true). If two stars have the same brightness, then the one closer to Earth appears brighter.

The only direct way of measuring the distance to the stars was first used successfully by German astronomer Friedrich Bessel in the 1830s. Bessel's method makes use of the parallax effect—the way that a nearby object appears to change its position against a more distant background when the observer's point of view changes.

A time-exposure image captures the bright stars in and around the constellation Orion. Brightest of all is Sirius, the Dog Star (far left). The dotted line on the bottom left is the movement of a satellite.

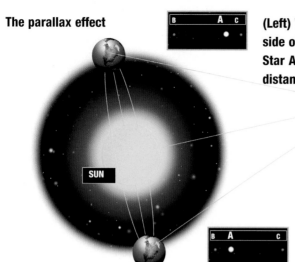

The parallax effect

(Left) When viewed from one side of Earth's orbit, the near Star A appears closer to the distant Star C.

A

(Above, right) When viewed from the other side of Earth's orbit, Star A appears closer to Star B.

See for yourself how the parallax effect works: Hold your arm out, close one eye, and look at your thumb. Now switch eyes and look at your thumb again. Your thumb seems to change its location slightly when viewed with your left or right eye.

All stars are so far away from Earth that any parallax effect is tiny. Fortunately, Earth's orbit provides two hugely separated viewpoints: Every six months, Earth moves 186 million miles (300 million kilometers) around the Sun. While this distance is tiny compared to Earth's distance to the stars, it is large enough for astronomers to detect and measure.

Bessel first measured the parallax effect using the double star 61 Cygni, which proved to be some 10.3 light-years away. One light-year (*see box, page 8*) equals 6 trillion miles (10 trillion km). From this measurement, Bessel determined that the 61 Cygni pair shines with just one-sixth the brightness of the Sun. Astronomers have measured the distances to millions of other stars using this method—most recently using

THE ELECTROMAGNETIC SPECTRUM

Light that we see is only a small part of the electromagnetic (EM) spectrum—the mostly invisible radiation, or energy, given off by stars. Electromagnetic radiation takes the form of different wavelengths of energy as it travels across the universe. All wavelengths of the EM spectrum move at the same speed: the speed of light—186,000 miles (300,000 km) per second.

The visible part of the EM spectrum, in the middle, ranges from red light with longer wavelengths, to violet light with shorter wavelengths. Beyond the visible violet light, the wavelengths become increasingly short, high-energy wavelengths that give off dangerous ionizing, or "hot," radiation such as ultraviolet rays, X-rays, and gamma rays. Likewise, the wavelengths beyond red light become increasingly long, with lower energy levels, such as infrared (heat) waves, microwaves, radar waves, and radio waves.

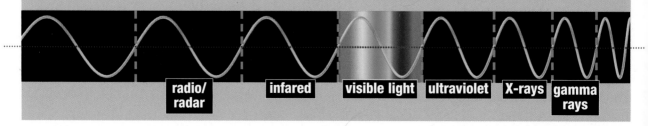

radio/radar — infared — visible light — ultraviolet — X-rays — gamma rays

sophisticated orbital observatories such as the *Hipparcos* satellite. They discovered that our nearest stellar neighbors are just a few light-years away. The most distant stars, however, are many thousands of light-years away—so distant that they show no parallax at all.

Variations in brightness

Distance measurements allow us to determine the true luminosities of stars. Just because a star is very bright in the sky, it does not always mean that the star is close to Earth. While it is true that some of the brightest stars are Earth's close neighbors, other stars that appear very bright are, in fact, unimaginably distant. There are also dim "dwarf" stars that are very close to us but are simply too faint to detect. In general, it seems that the brightness of stars ranges from one hundred thousand times brighter than our Sun, to one hundred thousand times dimmer.

MEASURING BRIGHTNESS

Astronomers measure the luminosity, or overall energy output, of a star— what we call its brightness—using two terms: apparent magnitude and absolute magnitude. Apparent magnitude measures how bright a star appears to the naked eye. Absolute magnitude, meanwhile, is a standardized measure used worldwide by astrophysicists and other professional astronomers. They calculate a star's absolute magnitude using a distance unit called the parsec (1 parsec equals 3.26 light-years), which is based on the geometric properties of a right triangle and the positions of Earth on either side of the Sun, the Sun itself, and the star in question. This method assumes that all stars are the same distance from Earth, which makes it easy to compare brightnesses.

Stars are graded according to luminosity, from magnitude 1.0 (brightest) to magnitude 6.0 (faintest). Modern telescopes detect millions of stars, so now the magnitude scale extends into negative numbers for the brightest stars. (Sirius, the brightest of all, is magnitude -1.4).

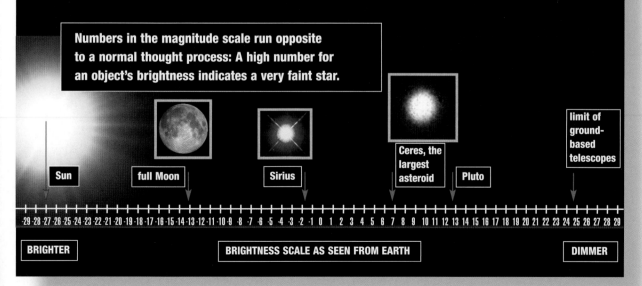

Numbers in the magnitude scale run opposite to a normal thought process: A high number for an object's brightness indicates a very faint star.

Sun

full Moon

Sirius

Ceres, the largest asteroid

Pluto

limit of ground-based telescopes

-29 -28 -27 -26 -25 -24 -23 -22 -21 -20 -19 -18 -17 -16 -15 -14 -13 -12 -11 -10 -9 -8 -7 -6 -5 -4 -3 -2 -1 0 1 2 3 4 5 6 7 8 9 10 11 12 13 14 15 16 17 18 19 20 21 22 23 24 25 26 27 28 29

BRIGHTER

BRIGHTNESS SCALE AS SEEN FROM EARTH

DIMMER

ASTRONOMICAL DISTANCES

Stars and galaxies are so far away that astronomers cannot use miles or kilometers to measure them—if they gave these figures, they would contain so many 0s at the end they would be meaningless! Interstellar distances are usually given in light-years instead. A light-year is simply the distance traveled by light in one year (*see page 13*). In other words, the distance of an object in light-years indicates how long its light takes to reach Earth. For comparison, light from the Sun takes eight-and-one-half light minutes to get to Earth.

Professional astronomers, meanwhile, more commonly use parsecs to measure distances. One parsec (short for parallax second) is the distance that a star appears to move because of the parallax effect. (1 parsec equals 3.26 light-years.)

Color, size, and mass

At first glance, the stars in the sky appear white because the human eye cannot distinguish color in faint objects. In fact, stars are found in colors ranging from red, through orange, yellow, and white, to blue. There are even a few stars that appear greenish in color. These different colors tell us a great deal about the physical properties of stars, and combined with measurements of their true luminosities, can reveal even more.

The reason behind the different colors is simple enough—the surface temperature of a star determines its color. Just as a metal bar heated in a furnace glows first red, then yellow, then white, and finally blue, so do stars. The colors of stars are generally less obvious because the star

**4,000 °Fahrenheit
(2,200 °Celsius)**

**7,000 °F
(4,000 °C)**

GARNET STAR

This star in the constellation Cepheus is one of the reddest in the sky. A red supergiant, its surface is relatively cool and red because of its enormous size. The garnet star is found about 2,800 light-years from Earth.

HAMAL

The brightest star in the constellation Aries is a yellow giant. Far more luminous than our Sun, Hamal has a similar color because of its larger diameter. Hamal lies 75 light-years from Earth.

is usually pouring out light wavelengths of every color, which combine to create white light.

The temperature of the surface of the star also affects how intense the color of the star will be. Cool stars emit most of their energy at long wavelengths and give off red colors. Hot stars are able to emit more at short, high-energy wavelengths and so give off blue colors. Our star, the Sun, has a surface temperature of 9,900 °F (5,500 °C) and a yellowish tinge to its light. Slightly hotter stars such as Sirius—the brightest star in our sky, with a surface temperature about 18,000 °F (10,000 °C)—tends to appear white.

But what controls a star's surface temperature? Here, astronomers make a series of connections that allow them to learn about the star's size from its color and luminosity.

A star is only heated by the energy inside itself, which passes out through the star's surface. The surface temperature and color are determined by two factors—the star's overall energy output (its luminosity) and the star's overall surface area (its size). A large star will provide a much larger surface area for the internal energy to pass through than a small star. This means a large star will appear cooler and redder than a small star of the same luminosity.

Star types

Understanding the facts about the luminosities and colors of stars in this way allows us to get a real picture of the stars—and reveals a crowded and confusing zoo of different star types. These include:

Sunlike stars: Stars with a similar luminosity and color to the Sun, which means they have a surface temperature of a few thousand degrees.

Red giants: Stars many times brighter than the Sun, but with much cooler surfaces, suggesting that the process that makes them brighter also

Pictured below are some stars visible with the naked eye, placed on a scale showing their relative surface temperature and their color. The surface temperature of Algol, a blue-white binary star, is ten times hotter than the Garnet Star.

11,000 °F (6,000 °C)	14,000 °F (8,000 °C)	18,000 °F (10,000 °C)	36,000 °F (20,000 °C)

CAPELLA
One of the brightest stars in the sky, Capella is actually a close pair of large, yellow-white stars, 46 light-years away.

ALPHECCA
The brightest star in the constellation Corona Borealis is blue-white. Alphecca lies 75 light-years from Earth.

ALGOL
Second-brightest in the constellation Perseus, Algol is a binary variable. Its combined brightness changes as the two stars eclipse each other's light as they orbit.

causes them to swell to enormous size, perhaps larger than the orbit of Earth around the Sun.

Blue giants: Stars far more luminous than the Sun, but also bluer, indicating that some factors can cause stars to shine far more brightly while keeping their size roughly the same.

Red dwarfs: Faint stars in our stellar neighborhood, whose energy output is too feeble to heat their surfaces much.

White dwarfs: Stars that are faint but also white, suggesting that they are releasing modest mounts of energy through a tiny surface area, hardly any larger than Earth's.

Putting it all together

So far, we've looked at the individual characteristics of stars, including their distance, luminosity, surface temperature, size, and mass.

The result is a wide range of different star types, but how are they related, and what story are they telling? The only way to find out is to study them statistically—by looking at the numbers of different types of stars and the relationships between them.

But there are some factors to bear in mind. One is that stars have very long, slow lives: We cannot usually watch a star change from one type to another in a few years or even decades, so we only see a "snapshot" of different stars at various stages of their lives. Another factor is

White dwarf stars can be far hotter than the Sun, but because they have a much smaller surface to emit light, they appear very faint. This diagram shows the size of a typical white dwarf compared to the Sun and Earth.

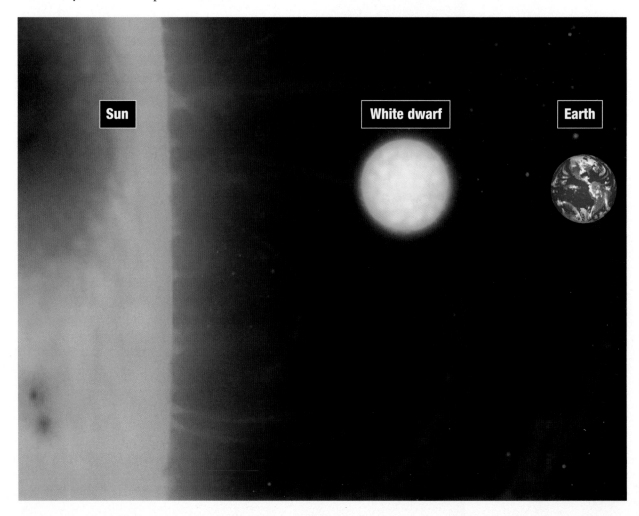

Sun

White dwarf

Earth

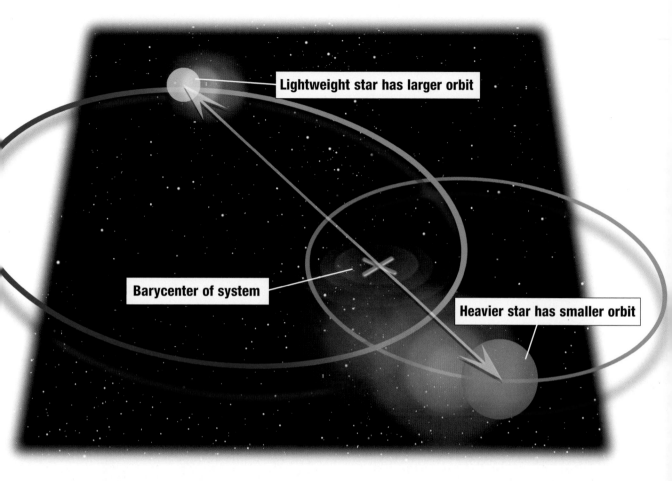

Lightweight star has larger orbit

Barycenter of system

Heavier star has smaller orbit

The distance of two stars from their common center of gravity ("barycenter") reveals their relative weights.

STAR WEIGHTS

Astronomers cannot weigh a star, so they use what they know about gravity and how it affects objects in our solar system to calculate estimates of other stars. An equation that was devised by Isaac Newton uses Johannes Kepler's Third Law to determine the masses of celectial objects in orbit. By studying the orbit of a star, including its distance from the barycenter (center of gravity for that system), its orbital path, and how long it takes for one orbit, astronomers get an idea of that star's weight. For binary star systems, this method is fairly easy, since the two stars orbit around that system's barycenter. Once astronomers know a star's orbit, they can calculate how massive that star would need to be to produce those particular gravitational effects.

that the stars we see are the brightest and the nearest. Distant, faint stars are simply beyond the range of even the best telescopes.

Astronomers categorize stars by comparing surface temperatures to brightnesses, which reveals clear relationships between the two.

When placed in the "Hertzprung-Russel" diagram, stars cluster around a line called the main sequence. This line shows that, for nearly all stars—from bright blue ones to dim red ones—greater luminosity is linked to higher surface temperature. The sequence diminishes

OBSERVING ACROSS THE SPECTRUM

Only a small fraction of electromagnetic (EM) radiation from space reaches the surface of Earth. Although our planet's atmosphere absorbs most of the ultraviolet (UV) and some of the infrared (IR) and radio wavelengths, the visible portion of the EM spectrum makes it to the ground intact. We feel the IR radiation that penetrates the atmosphere as the Sun's heat on our bodies and other objects, while the UV rays that get through often produce skin damage, including tanning or sunburn. Still, the atmosphere also protects us from the more dangerous and damaging EM wavelengths, including X-rays and gamma rays.

We use the different wavelengths of the EM spectrum to explore space. Most ground-based telescopes scan the universe using visible light. For the clearest views, they are often located on mountaintops, where Earth's atmosphere is thinnest. On these mountain peaks, special IR telescopes also detect some of the IR radiation before the denser parts of our atmosphere block it. The best IR observing occurs from space-based telescopes, not only because of the lack of atmospheric blocking, but also because of the lack of ambient heat generated by Earth and by the IR telescope itself—which can distort images. The cold temperatures of space also require less refrigerant for cooling an orbiting IR telescope.

Earth-based radio telescopes, like the famous one in Arecibo, Puerto Rico, consist of huge metal dishes that collect long-wavelength radio waves from space. Smaller versions of radio telescopes, often built in movable groups called arrays, allow astronomers to combine many separate radio images into one larger image. Additionally, space-based radio telescopes collect and beam such data to Earth.

Space-based telescopes capable of studying the universe in different wavelengths became a reality in the decades after the launch of *Sputnik,* the world's first artificial satellite. While the famous *Hubble Space Telescope (HST)* collects images in visible light, it also carries equipment that scans the universe in IR—as does the *Spitzer Space Telescope (Spitzer).* Space-based UV instruments include the *Hopkins Ultraviolet Telescope,* used by space shuttle astronauts, the *Cosmic Hot Interstellar Plasma Spectrometer (CHIPS),* and the *Far Ultraviolet Spectroscopic Explorer (FUSE)* Mission. The *Wilkinson Microwave Anisotropy Probe (WMAP)* studies and maps the background microwave radiation of the universe. Space-based X-ray detectors include the *Rossi X-ray Timing Explorer* Mission, and the *XMM-Newton* and *Chandra* X-ray observatories, while the *High Energy Transient Explorer-2 (HETE-2)* Mission and *International Gamma-Ray Astrophysics Laboratory (INTEGRAL)* detect gamma-ray wavelengths. Telescopes dedicated to short-wavelength EM radiation are built to prevent these high-energy rays from simply passing right through them.

The "Hertzsprung-Russell diagram" reveals clear patterns in the properties of stars—the vast majority lie along a band called the main sequence, suggesting that most stars spend most of their lives in a stable state. Giants are relatively common. Toward the end of their lives, most stars pass through a giant phase. Supergiants are rare, and dwarfs are also rare, mostly because they are hard to detect.

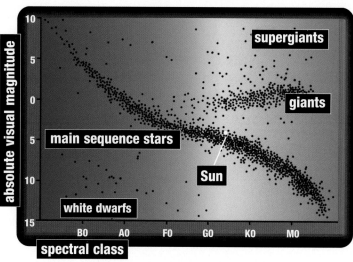

at either end, for different reasons. Bright blue stars, while truly rare, are still obvious even over great distances. Dim red stars appear to be rare simply because of the limitations of current telescopes. Our Sun sits squarely in the middle of the main sequence, a yellow-white star of average brightness.

The exceptions to the main sequence occur less frequently, but they, too, fall into clear groupings: red giants (highly luminous but cool stars to the right of the main sequence) and white dwarfs (faint but hot stars to the bottom-left of the main sequence). Along the top of the diagram are found the extremely brilliant stars of various colors. Such "supergiants" are the largest of the known stars, with the red supergiants the very largest of all.

Measuring tool

Astronomers analyze the light emitted by giants and dwarfs to distinguish them from "normal" stars in the main sequence. The main sequence can also be used as a tool for estimating the distances of stars. If we know a main-sequence star's type and color, we can place it on the main sequence, figure out its likely luminosity, and then find its distance by the size it appears to be in Earth's skies.

The distribution of stars on such a diagram tells us a great deal about the lives of stars. It suggests, above all, that the vast majority maintain the same brightness and color throughout their lives. They

only change toward the end of their lives. To put together a real picture of how stars evolve, we need to understand how stars generate their energy. This is something twentieth-century astronomers managed to discover by studying our local star, the Sun.

THE SPEED OF LIGHT

All electromagnetic (EM) radiation travels through the vacuum of space at exactly the same speed—186,000 miles (300,000 km) per second. Most often, we call this the speed of light. (What we call "light" is the visible portion of the radiation of different wavelengths that make up the EM spectrum.)

In his 1905 Special Theory of Relativity, Einstein's famous equation mathematically proved that nothing could travel faster than the speed of light. For this reason, we use the speed of light as a "constant"—a unit that never changes. One light-year is the distance light travels in one Earth year, which is roughly 6 trillion miles (10 trillion km). It is a convenient way of measuring the huge distances in space. In other words, a light-year measures distances, not time.

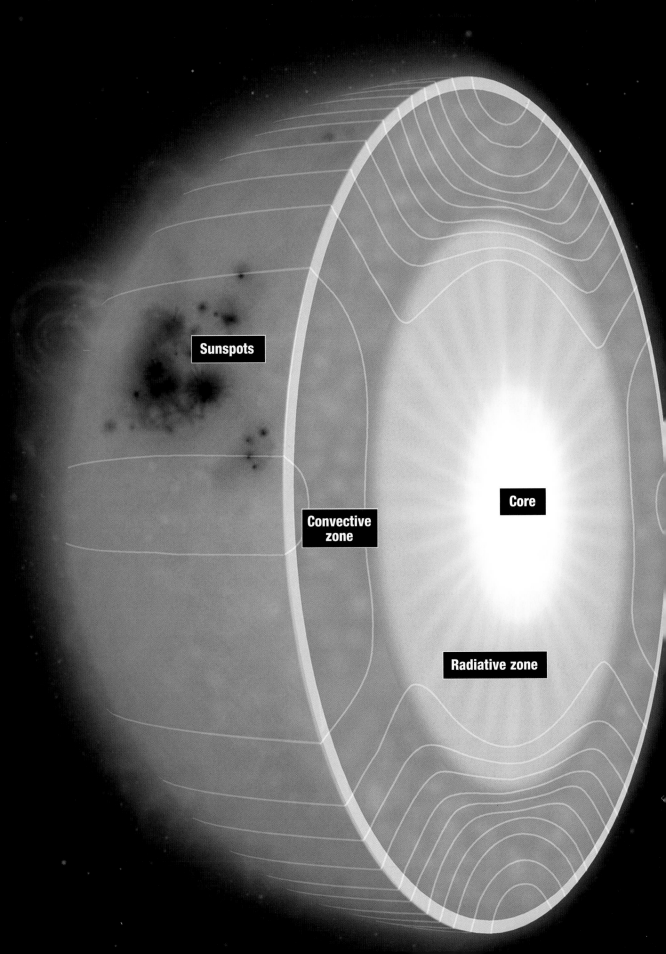

THE SUN

Sitting on our cosmic doorstep just 93 million miles (150 million km) away, the Sun is the only star we can study in detail. Much of what we understand about other stars comes from our discoveries of how the Sun operates.

The Sun is a huge ball of gas, dominated by the gas hydrogen but with significant amounts of helium. Deep inside, the sheer amount of material pulled together under the Sun's own gravity creates enormous pressures and temperatures, which are far higher than the 9,900 °F (5,500 °C) of the solar surface. This visible surface of the Sun, called the photosphere, is some 865,000 miles (1,400,000 km) across. The Sun does not have an actual surface such as that found on a rocky planet. The photosphere simply marks the region in which the Sun's gases become transparent and from which energy, in the form of light rays and other types of radiation, escapes freely. Beyond the photosphere, a thin but hot outer atmosphere called the corona stretches millions of miles further. This eventually blends in with the "solar wind," a stream of particles from the Sun that radiate out across the entire solar system.

Within the Sun, hydrogen gas, which is normally found as a molecule containing two atoms joined together, is separated into individual atoms. Normally, each atom consists of a nucleus, where most of its mass is concentrated, orbited by a tiny lightweight, negatively charged electron. In hydrogen's case, the nucleus contains one positively charged particle called a proton, but the temperatures inside the Sun are so great that the electron is stripped away. This leaves the positively charged hydrogen nuclei exposed to collisions with other nuclei, which is the key to energy production inside the Sun. The same thing happens with slightly heavier helium (*see upper box, page 21*).

Just as geologists study earthquake shockwaves to determine the structure of Earth, astronomers use waves passing through the Sun to unlock its secrets. Solar shockwaves reveal the Sun's three major layers: the core, the radiative zone, and the convective zone.

Surface features

Everyone knows that, because of its sheer brilliance, if you look directly at the Sun you risk permanently damaging your eyes. This fierce blaze of light also drowns out details of the Sun's surface, so it just appears to be a featureless disk. Astronomers have devised some ways of safely looking at and photographing the Sun's surface (*see box, page 17*), which has revealed an astonishing amount of activity. The most obvious are dark blotches on the Sun's surface, known as sunspots. These mark areas where the photosphere is cooler than average. Although their temperature is still approximately 6,300 °F (3,500 °C), they appear dark in comparison to the surrounding hotter regions. Sunspot groups come and go in periods ranging from days to weeks. Because they are carried

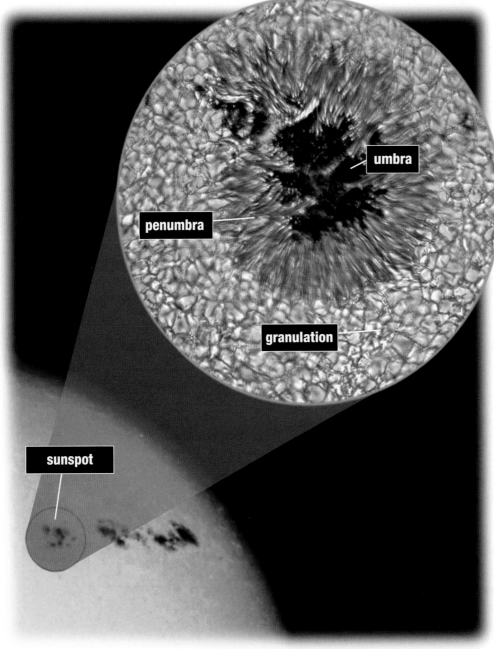

umbra

penumbra

granulation

sunspot

Zooming in on a sunspot reveals a pattern that looks similar to the ones made by iron filings pulled around by a magnet. Both patterns are formed by magnetic fields. A sunspot typically has a dark, dense "umbra" surrounded by a broader, fainter "penumbra."

around by the Sun's rotation, the longest-lived ones can survive the period when they are not visible to us, disappearing from one edge (or "limb") of the Sun's disk and reappearing some time later on the other. By measuring how long it takes for a sunspot to reappear, astronomers can tell how fast the Sun is rotating. The answer is surprising. Regions close to the Sun's poles rotate in about thirty-five days, while those near the equator spin in twenty-five days. When this fact was first discovered, this type of motion, called "differential rotation," was important evidence that the Sun was not a solid object.

Sunspots are cool because the gases within them are less dense than in the surrounding regions. The lower density is caused by loops of the Sun's powerful magnetic field emerging through the photosphere. Because the loop emerges through the photosphere in one place and reenters it in another, sunspots are usually found in pairs. Another feature on the Sun's surface are blobs called faculae. These bright blobs on the Sun's surface are smaller areas where magnetic fields are more concentrated than in their surroundings. These are less obvious than the sunspots because they are bright.

Granules and supergranules

Underlying all these features is a pattern called granulation. Astronomers found that, when viewed with special filters, the Sun's surface looks like a mosaic of bright spots with dark borders, each about 600 miles (1,000 km) across. These granules are constantly moving and reforming. They mark the tops of convection cells, where hot and bright material welling up from inside the Sun cools, is forced aside by more upwelling material, cools again, and drops back into the interior. The granules themselves join together in larger supergranules.

Along the edges of the supergranules, bright protrusions that look like flames, called spicules, erupt into the upper atmosphere for 6,000 miles (10,000 km) or more.

OBSERVING THE SUN

Never look at the Sun through a telescope or binoculars. One of the few safe ways of looking at the Sun is by projecting its image through a telescope onto a piece of card. Professional astronomers and serious amateur observers also use special solar filters that clamp over the front of their telescopes and block out all but a few key wavelengths of the Sun's light. Some manufacturers sell solar filters that attach to a telescope's eyepiece. These are dangerous, however, and should never be used because the sunlight focused by the telescope could cause the filter to crack and shatter suddenly. Even so-called "eclipse glasses" can be dangerous if they are scratched or if you try to look at the Sun through them for too long.

A card held in line with the eyepiece of this telescope captures a large, clear image of the Sun and its features. The image on the card is completely safe to view.

Solar outbursts

The Sun is a violent place, and material often escapes from the photosphere into the corona. Small outbursts called prominences are seen on a regular basis, often above regions of sunspot activity. Relatively cool, they appear as reddish loops of gas above the limb of the Sun's disk, and are visible to the naked eye during total solar eclipses. Their looping shapes arise as they follow the same solar magnetic field loops that cause sunspots. Prominences seen against the brighter backdrop of the photosphere appear as dark streaks called "filaments."

Solar flares

A prominence is very impressive, but another even more amazing activity, known as the solar flare, takes place on the surface of the Sun. Solar flares occur in huge bursts when the Sun ejects gas and particles into interplanetary space at speeds of millions of miles an hour. When the material from a flare reaches Earth, it can be swept up by our planet's magnetic field and plunges into the atmosphere above the magnetic poles. This can disrupt power grids on Earth and often creates spectacular displays known as the northern and southern lights (also called auroras).

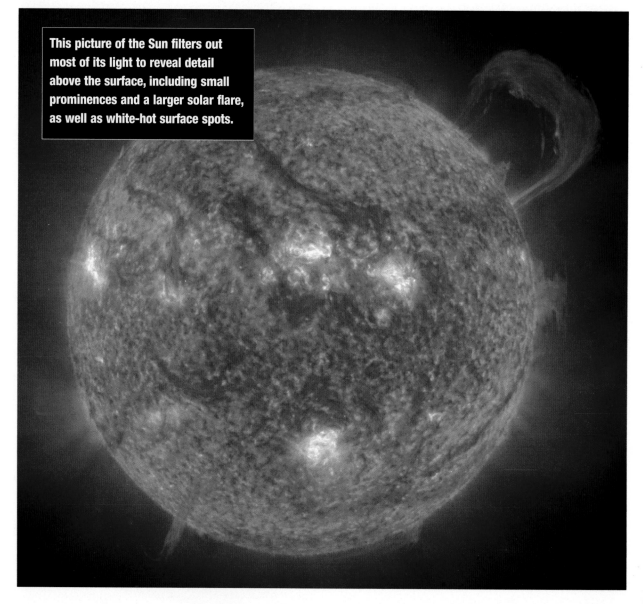

This picture of the Sun filters out most of its light to reveal detail above the surface, including small prominences and a larger solar flare, as well as white-hot surface spots.

The Solar Cycle

Solar activity, from sunspots to flares, fluctuates from year to year. Records of the number of sunspots and their positions reveal a pattern to these variations that seems to last roughly eleven years. Astronomers have since realized that the true cycle is actually twenty-two years long, and it is linked to the creation and destruction of the Sun's magnetic field.

A typical solar cycle starts when the Sun is in a relatively quiet phase. New sunspots appear at latitudes of about 35 degrees—comparatively close to the North and South poles—and drift closer to the Sun's equator over several weeks' time. Over the course of several years, the overall number of sunspots increases. Other solar activity, such as flares, prominences, and magnetic particles ejections that cause auroras on Earth, rises along with sunspot numbers. As the sunspots approach the solar equator, their numbers begin to diminish, and the Sun becomes less active. Finally, the sunspots disappear completely, and the Sun returns to its placid phase.

When sunspots eventually return at high solar latitudes, their polarities (north-south alignments) are reversed, indicating that the Sun's entire magnetic field has flipped. This only happens because the Sun's magnetic field is not like that of a planet. Instead, it is the combination of magnetism caused by all the individual masses of gas circulating within the Sun's interior. At the start of a solar cycle, the Sun's magnetic field is like that of a planet or a bar magnet, exiting the photosphere at the Sun's poles, and elsewhere running "within" the star.

Over time, however, the Sun's "differential rotation" messes up the alignment, and the magnetic field becomes tangled. Loops of the field begin to protrude through the photosphere, forming sunspots and allowing other activity to begin. The loops emerge first at high latitude, but gradually increase in numbers and get closer to the equator. As they near the equator, the loops start to connect across it, canceling each other out and destroying the Sun's magnetic field completely.

THE LITTLE ICE AGE

The solar cycle isn't always reliable. In the early 2000s there was a mysterious "double peak," with activity suddenly returning when astronomers thought it should be falling away.

More famously, between 1645 and 1715, sunspot activity disappeared completely. At the same time, Earth seems to have gone through a "Little Ice Age," with cold summers and exceptionally cold winters. The coincidence of a minimum number of sunspots and the Little Ice Age is strong evidence that the solar cycle affects Earth's weather.

This print commemorates a "frost fair" held on London's River Thames when it froze over in 1684, partly due to the Little Ice Age.

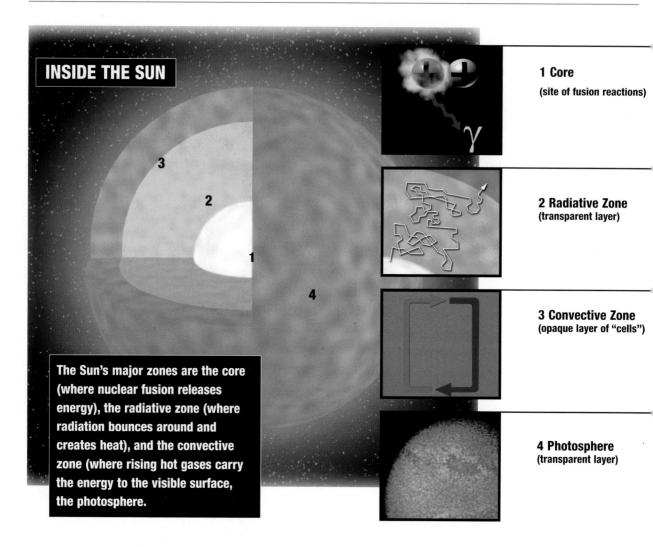

INSIDE THE SUN

3
2
1
4

1 Core
(site of fusion reactions)

γ

2 Radiative Zone
(transparent layer)

3 Convective Zone
(opaque layer of "cells")

4 Photosphere
(transparent layer)

The Sun's major zones are the core (where nuclear fusion releases energy), the radiative zone (where radiation bounces around and creates heat), and the convective zone (where rising hot gases carry the energy to the visible surface, the photosphere.

When it reappears, the former magnetic north pole is now the south pole.

Inside the Sun

Beneath the photosphere, the Sun consists of three major layers. The central core occupies about one-quarter of the Sun's diameter. Then comes the radiative zone, stretching to two-thirds of the way out. The outermost layer is the convective zone. Stretching from the boundary of the radiative zone to the surface, the convective zone is 140,000 miles (225,000 km) thick.

The core of the Sun—the power source that has allowed it to shine unchanged for billions of years—holds its greatest mystery. Astronomers used to think that the Sun's power was caused by the Sun contracting because of gravity. But this could only power a weak star for a few million years. Ever since the early twentieth century, geologists have known that Earth itself is several billion years old.

We now know that the Sun is powered by nuclear fusion, a type of nuclear reaction in which the nuclei of light atoms are forced together to form heavier ones. The main fusion reaction that happens in the Sun is called the proton-proton (p-p) chain. In this, positively charged subatomic particles called protons (the central nuclei of hydrogen) collide with one another to form the atomic nuclei of the heavier and more complex atom, helium. In the process, a small amount of excess mass is converted directly into a large amount of energy, released in the form of short-wavelength gamma rays.

PROTON–PROTON CHAIN

1 Two free protons fuse to form a new nucleus.

2 Another free proton fuses with the new nucleus to form an unstable helium-3 nucleus; nuclear energy is released.

3 Two helium-3 nuclei fuse to form a stable helium-4 nucleus; two free protons are released.

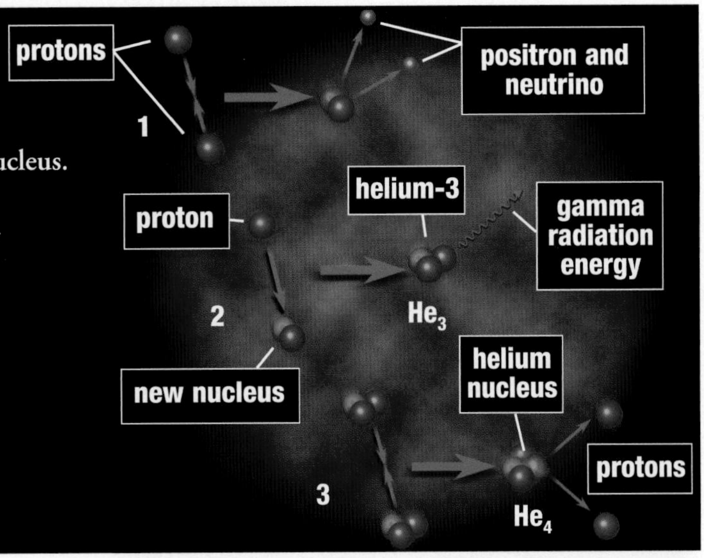

protons

positron and neutrino

1

proton

helium-3

gamma radiation energy

2

He$_3$

new nucleus

helium nucleus

protons

3

He$_4$

On Earth, such rays can penetrate through almost any material, but the interior of the Sun is so dense and packed with atoms that the gamma rays are constantly colliding with the material there. As the gamma rays leave the core, they ricochet around the radiative zone (*see illustration above*), transferring much of their energy to the material around them, and keeping the zone incredibly hot. Because the ricocheting gamma rays travel randomly, they take a long time—up to 100,000 years—to make their way through that layer.

Convective zone

Throughout the radiative zone, the Sun is transparent. At the bottom of the convective zone, the sun suddenly becomes opaque. It cannot transmit radiation, so the escaping energy must find a new way to reach the surface. Gas at the bottom of the zone absorbs the energy, heats up and expands, pushing its way up through its cooler surroundings, toward the photosphere, creating a convection cell. At the photosphere, the Sun becomes transparent again, and the convection gases radiate their excess energy, mostly in the form of visible light. The cooling gas falls back down around the edges of each convection cell, forming the darker granule edges.

SPECTROSCOPY

Spectroscopy is the science of studying the different wavelengths of light sources. A prism splits sunlight into a spectrum of colors corresponding to many different wavelengths. Dark lines at certain points in the Sun's spectrum mark gaps where specific wavelengths are blocked. The gaps represent "absorption lines" that indicate which elements in the Sun are absorbing those wavelengths. The unique set of dark lines on the spectrum of any celestial object acts as a "fingerprint" that lets us identify which elements that object contains. Astronomers can determine the composition, temperature, and density of an object by analyzing its spectrum.

Spectrum diagram showing the absorption lines of hydrogen, the most common element in the universe.

Artist's impression of a young star. Material from the protostellar nebula is still falling into it and is blasted out in jets from the star's poles.

LIFE STORIES

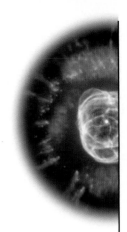

By combining their understanding of processes inside the Sun with their models of how different types of stars are distributed and related to one another, astronomers have pieced together a detailed model of the life stories of stars. Every star in the sky fits somewhere into this grand scheme, but exactly where depends on the star's age, its chemical composition, and its mass.

Star birth

Stars are born in great clouds of gas and dust called nebulae that hang between the stars. Some nebulae are visible, glowing with the heat of radiation from nearby stars, or they simply shine with reflected light. Most are dark, however, and are only detected where they are seen in silhouette against a brighter background. It is in these dark clouds that the process of a star's birth

ARTHUR EDDINGTON

British astronomer Sir Arthur Eddington (1882–1944) was a major influence on our modern picture of stellar evolution. Working at Cambridge in the 1920s, he had the idea of comparing the positions of stars with their masses. This revealed that the more massive a star is, the brighter it is during its main-sequence lifetime. This relationship between mass and luminosity held the key to explaining the positions of stars in astronomical diagrams.

Eddington also made detailed calculations of the conditions inside stars, discovering the links between luminosity, color, and size. He was also the first person to suggest that nuclear fusion powered the stars.

begins. As nebulae travel through space, they sometimes begin to collapse. A number of factors, including shockwaves from a nearby supernova explosion, the gravity of a passing star, or the passage through a region of greater or lesser density can trigger this collapse.

When a nebula begins to collapse, it becomes what is called a protostellar cloud ("proto" means "beginning" and "stellar" means "star"). When a protostellar cloud collapses, it begins to spin. The collapse and spinning starts slowly, but feeds on its own acceleration. Slight movements that were already taking place in the cloud increase as material becomes more tightly packed, just as an ice-skater spins more rapidly when she pulls her arms inward.

As the protostellar cloud becomes denser, it separates from the general material around it, forming a dark ball called a proplyd. Individual stars rarely form on their own, so proplyds born from the collapse of the same dark nebula often cluster together. More often than not, they begin to orbit around each other. That is why single stars, such as the Sun, actually seem to be less common than binary (pairs) of stars or multiples (groups) of stars.

Fusion begins

Within each proplyd, a dense core or protostar begins forming, heating up as its closely packed gas atoms collide. Eventually, the protostar begins to radiate heat and light. The heavier it becomes, the faster it pulls in the material around it. The remaining gas and dust, meanwhile, that flatten out into a broad disk around the young star may eventually give birth to a system of planets, moons, asteroids, and comets. As the proplyd begins to "dissolve," the young star emerges from its cocoon. When its core reaches "critical" density and temperature—when conditions are just right for fusion reactions to begin—the pressure of radiation blasting out through the star holds it up against further collapse. At this point, the star may go through some violent pulsations and throw off material sucked in from its surrounding disk in jets through its poles. Before long, the brand-new star settles down to produce a steady luminosity and surface temperature.

Dust and gas coalesce inside a protostellar nebula. While the core becomes hotter and collapses into a protostar, cooler material in orbit around it may eventually form planets.

MULTIPLE STARS

Because they are born in clusters within nebulae, stars often form in orbit around each another. The most common multiple stars are pairs—so-called "binary" stars—but systems with three, four, or even more stars in orbit (known as multiple stars) are very common. All the stars in a multiple system orbit around their shared center of gravity, which allows astronomers to determine their relative weights from the size of their orbits (*see box, page 11*). Stars of different masses age at different rates, so it is not unusual to find systems where

stars are at different stages of evolution. Some of the most interesting cases are systems where the two stars are close together and one has evolved into a white dwarf, while the other has become a giant. The dwarf's strong gravity allows it to tug material from the outer layers of the giant star. As the layers build up around the star, they occasionally burn away in explosions called novae, from the Latin word for "new stars." This is a very appropriate name because the sudden brightening can cause stars to flare into visibility for the first time.

A small, dense white dwarf pulls material away from its larger, but less dense, companion in a nova system.

Stellar life spans

How long a star remains a main sequence star depends mainly on its mass, since this governs its density and core temperature. Stars like the Sun, with core temperatures of about 27 million °F (15 million °C) burn through the hydrogen in their cores in roughly ten billion years. Smaller stars burn even more slowly.

Stars of eight solar masses or more, however, burn their way through their fuel reserves much faster. Despite the fact that their cores contain far more hydrogen than stars like the Sun, they can use it all up in tens of millions of years. The high temperatures in their cores allow them to use a different type of nuclear fusion, called the CNO (carbon-nitrogen-oxygen) cycle.

The reaction still turns hydrogen into helium, but does it at a much faster rate, so the star shines brighter but burns out faster.

Red giants

No matter what type of fusion a star uses, it eventually converts all the hydrogen in its core to helium. At this point, the fusion process begins to move outward into an expanding spherical shell. This shell-burning phase boosts the star's energy output. As its luminosity increases, its outer layers balloon outward and then cool. By this process, the star becomes a red giant.

The abandoned core, meanwhile, collapses under its own gravity and grows steadily hotter. It reaches a point where it is so hot that a new type of fusion begins, combining helium nuclei to create carbon. As core energy is restored, the star's overall brightness actually drops, and the star shrinks.

Helium burning in a star like the Sun typically lasts for about two billion years. When the core's fuel supply is exhausted again, helium fusion moves out into a second shell as it follows the hydrogen fusion moving through the star's outer regions. The core gradually collapses, growing denser and hotter once again—but this marks the end of the road for a sunlike star.

In more massive stars, the core grows hot and dense enough for other new types of fusion to occur. Carbon and helium fuse together to form oxygen, and further reactions create neon, sodium, magnesium, sulfur, and other elements.

Each of these reactions uses up fuel more rapidly than the previous one. Each in turn moves out into a shell, so that eventually the star's inner regions develop a structure like an onion. Even massive stars cannot shine forever, though, and when the star begins to form iron in its core, its spectacular end is near.

Planetary nebulae and white dwarfs

A sunlike star reaches the end of its life when it can no longer burn helium in its core. As the helium- and hydrogen-burning shells move out from the core of the swollen red giant, the star

VARIABLE STARS

Not all stars in the sky shine with a constant light. Many stars change their appearance over days or years. Sometimes this is a result of the arrangement of the star system itself, but at other times, the star is passing through an unstable phase of its life. A star changes its appearances most as it evolves off the main sequence and becomes a red giant or supergiant.

Some variable stars change their brightness very suddenly—these are usually eclipsing binaries, where the stars in a binary system happen to pass in front of each other as seen from Earth. Such stars might first appear as a single star, but when one passes in front of the other, it "eclipses" (temporarily blocks) the other, and the total amount of light reaching us from the system drops abruptly.

Some stars vary in brightness as they rotate. This may be because a massive companion in a binary system is pulling them out of shape or because they have huge "starspots" on their surface.

Most variable stars change in brightness as they pulsate. They are easy to detect because their brightness is constantly

becomes more and more unstable. Rapid expansion alternates with sudden contractions as the fusion process reaches areas where the density and temperature are too low to sustain them. The star's outer layers are flung off into space, leaving a glowing halo of gas around the dying star. This halo is known as a planetary nebula because it resembles the ghostly disk of a planet.

Stellar remnant

Within a relatively short span of time—perhaps a few thousand years—the star's outer layers are blown away completely. Soon they fade away to invisibility, and all that remains is the burned-out core of the star. With no nuclear reactions generating radiation to support it, the core collapses until it is a few thousand miles across and cannot collapse any further.

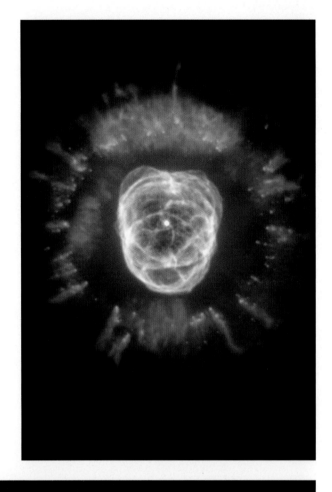

The shells of gas in planetary nebulae often form elaborate shapes. The Eskimo Nebula (NGC 2392), discovered by William Herschel in 1787, looks like someone wearing a parka.

changing. The different types of variable are named after their "prototype" star—the first one of that kind to be discovered.

In some types of pulsating variables, the period of pulsation is directly linked to the star's luminosity: The brighter the star, the longer its period.

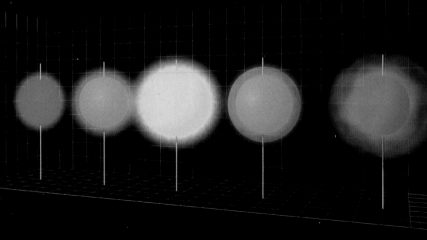

A pulsating variable star changes its size, brightness, and color in a repeating cycle.

By this point, matter in the star is so compressed that a teaspoon of it would weigh a ton. Although tiny for a star, this Earth-sized stellar remnant is still intensely hot, with a surface temperature about 180,000 °F (100,000 °C). It emits brilliant white light, but is so small that it is still very faint. In other words, it has become a white dwarf.

The ultimate fate of all stars like the Sun is to become a slowly cooling star remnant, drifting forever in space, and gradually fading away to become a truly dead black dwarf.

Supernovae, neutron stars, and black holes

Massive stars meet their blazing deaths when all the material in their core is converted to iron. But iron requires more energy for its fusion than it releases, so when the star attempts the fusion of iron nuclei, its power source abruptly cuts out. In a fraction of a second, the layers of the star collapse inward, hit the core, and tear themselves apart as a powerful shockwave ripples out through the star. Temperatures and pressures are briefly raised so high that the star blazes out with millions of times its previous luminosity. A supernova of this type can outshine its entire galaxy, but the display is brief. The star's shredded outer layers are scattered across space as a fiercely glowing supernova remnant, and the star itself fades away.

What remains is the remnant of a star far more mysterious than a white dwarf. When fusion ends in the star's core, the density of the iron is so high that even the pressure of repulsion between atomic nuclei cannot resist the force of gravity. The nuclei disintegrate into protons, with a positive electrical charge, and uncharged neutrons, and the protons combine with negative electron particles to form yet more neutrons. Eventually the pressure between individual neutrons becomes so great that the core's collapse comes to a halt. By this time, the star will have shrunk to a neutron star about the

size of a city, with a density so great that a single pinhead of its material would weigh 100,000 tons (91,000 tonnes).

In order to become a neutron star, the collapsing core must weigh more than 1.4 solar masses. This is the "Chandrasekhar limit," named after the Indian astronomer who first explained the nature of white dwarf stars. But even neutron stars turn out to have an upper limit on their weight. If the core is heavier than five Suns, then the pressure between neutrons is not strong enough to resist gravity, and the collapsing star continues to shrink. As it becomes ever more dense, the gravity at its surface grows stronger and stronger, until eventually not even light, the fastest thing in the universe, is able to escape it. The star has become a black hole, which is a tiny region of space that objects can only enter and never leave. At its heart lies the remains of the core, compressed to an infinitely dense point. This is known as a "singularity," and here the normal rules of space and time no longer apply.

Neutron star
Neutron stars are the densest form of matter that can exist—they form as the already dense core of a giant star is crushed by the pressures involved in a supernova explosion.

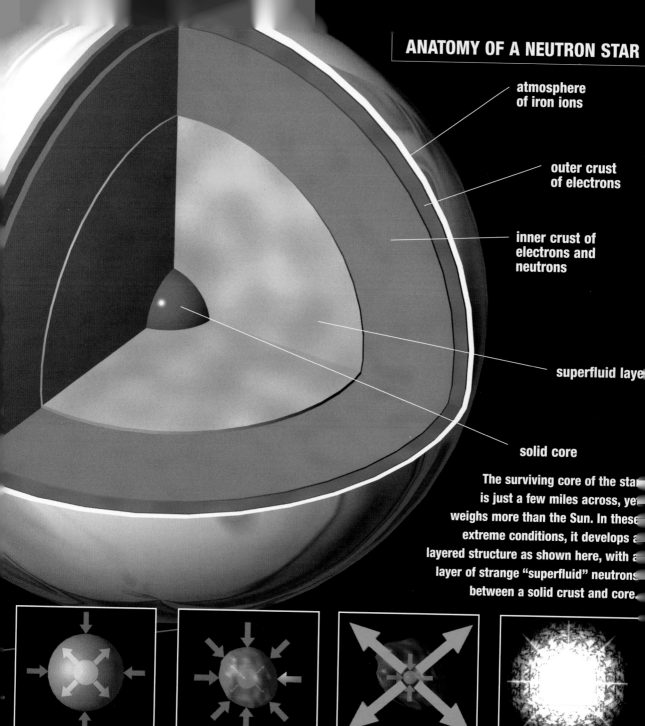

atmosphere
of iron ions

outer crust
of electrons

inner crust of
electrons and
neutrons

superfluid layer

solid core

The surviving core of the star
is just a few miles across, yet
weighs more than the Sun. In these
extreme conditions, it develops a
layered structure as shown here, with a
layer of strange "superfluid" neutrons
between a solid crust and core.

BALANCE

While fusion continues
in the core, outward
pressure of radiation
balances the weight of
the star's outer layers.

EXHAUSTION

When the star
attempts to fuse iron,
the outward pressure
drops rapidly, and the
star collapses inward.

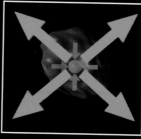

EXPLOSION

Collapsing layers
rebound off the
dense core, creating a
shockwave that travels
out through the star.

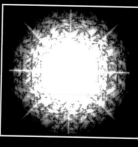

SUPERNOVA

The shockwaves
compress and heat
the star's outer layers
so that they detonate

CHAPTER 4

ANATOMY OF A GALAXY

All the stars in Earth's sky belong to our local galaxy, the Milky Way. When we see this diffuse band of stars (usually visible in the Northern Hemisphere on a dark summer night) stretching across the sky, we are actually seeing the combined light of millions of distant stars scattered across the plane of our galaxy. The Milky Way's true shape resembles a spiral. Its central hub bulges in the direction of the constellation Sagittarius.

Our place in the Milky Way

The solar system lies on the outer edge of the Milky Way's Orion Arm (spiral arms are named after the constellation in which they appear brightest). Our Sun and its planets sit about halfway between the central hub and the outer edge of the galaxy, some twenty-eight thousand light-years from the Milky Way's mysterious central region. Fortunately for life on

Earth, this is a relatively dull region of the galaxy in the middle of what some astronomers call the "galactic habitable zone." It's a location rich with heavy elements for planet formation, but far enough from the overcrowded and chaotic galactic center to avoid close encounters with nearby stars and supernovae.

The disk and spiral arms

The Milky Way measures one hundred thousand light-years across from edge to edge. Four major spiral arms (home to the brightest and youngest blue stars) emerge from the crowded central hub region and wrap nearly all the way around the galaxy. The space between the arms is littered with stars and clouds of gas and dust.

As the Milky Way spins through space, every object in it follows its own orbit around the center—so the galaxy does not rotate like a solid object. The Sun

This spectacular image of a "barred" spiral galaxy shows the concentration of older, yellow stars in the core. Dust, gas, and knots of bright young star formation mark the spiral arms.

Density lines represent the elliptical orbits of stars around a galaxy's center. The closely packed areas indicate where stars spend most of their time. Star tend to "pile up," creating a self-sustaining spiral pattern.

of the galaxy, they naturally move in and out of the density wave, just as drivers in a traffic jam behave to accommodate individual cars entering and leaving the freeway.

The density wave in a galaxy creates spiral regions that are more tightly packed than other parts of its disk. An object passing through the density wave triggers the collapse of dust and gas clouds, which sets off star formation. Galactic arms become full of dark clouds, emission nebulae, and bright blue stars. The life spans of the brightest stars are so short that they squander their fuel, swell to red supergiants, and detonate as supernovae in just a few million years. They simply do not survive long enough to move out of the spiral arm region, and so the brightest blue stars are always found in the arms. Shockwaves from the supernovae explosions of such giant stars, in turn, trigger new waves of star formation.

The arms and nearby regions also feature open clusters—loose groups of stars that have recently emerged from their nebulae and begun to shine as main sequence stars (*see pages 12–13*). Over tens of millions of years, these clusters tend to drift apart, and those stars that survive long enough will become scattered through the galactic disk. Our Sun has reached this stage. It formed long ago, but has completed many orbits around the galaxy since.

completes one orbit of the Milky Way galaxy every two hundred and fifty million years. Objects nearer to the center orbit complete their orbit much more quickly. The Milky Way is at least ten billion years old, and it has rotated many times in its life. So why haven't the spiral arms disappeared?

The arms will never disappear because they are not physical structures, but a result of the behavior of the material and forces existing within the entire orbiting system. The only feature that persists is a slowly rotating, spiral-shaped "density wave." In this region, objects move more slowly and become closely packed —somewhat like a celestial traffic jam on a galaxic freeway. As stars, gas, and dust clouds follow their individual orbits around the center

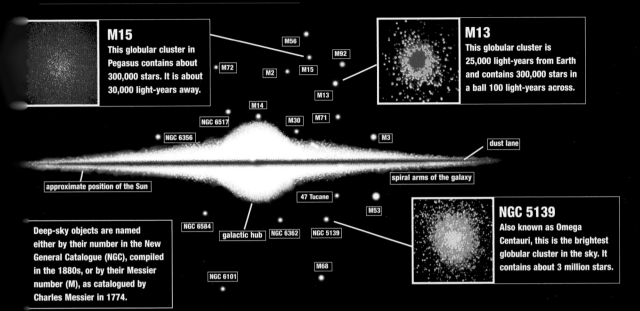

M15
This globular cluster in Pegasus contains about 300,000 stars. It is about 30,000 light-years away.

M13
This globular cluster is 25,000 light-years from Earth and contains 300,000 stars in a ball 100 light-years across.

M56

M92

M72

M2

M15

M13

M14

NGC 6517

M30

M71

NGC 6356

M3

dust lane

approximate position of the Sun

spiral arms of the galaxy

47 Tucane

M53

NGC 5139
Also known as Omega Centauri, this is the brightest globular cluster in the sky. It contains about 3 million stars.

Deep-sky objects are named either by their number in the New General Catalogue (NGC), compiled in the 1880s, or by their Messier number (M), as catalogued by Charles Messier in 1774.

NGC 6584

galactic hub

NGC 6362

NGC 5139

M68

NGC 6101

Many of the stars of the Milky Way cluster together, which signifies that they were probably all born in the same protostellar cloud. There are two distinct types of cluster—open and globular. Open clusters are found around the galaxy's spiral arms and contain anything from a few dozen to a few hundred young blue and white stars. Globular clusters are huge ball-shaped star clouds containing tens of thousands of old red and yellow stars that follow their own independent orbits around the center of the galaxy. They are often found above and below the plane of the galaxy in the 'halo' regions.

Open clusters consist of stars that are still huddled together following the events of their birth. Emission or reflection nebulae often surround them. Apart from those stars tied up in binary and multiple systems, most of the cluster members have their own motions

through space, and so the cluster will drift apart over millions of years, and its stars will be hard to distinguish from the background stars. For example, the Jewel Box cluster in the constellation Crux and the Pleiades in Taurus are both dense young clusters. Five of the well-spaced stars in the asterism we call the Big Dipper (in the constellation Ursa Major) belong to an open cluster that became scattered over time.

Globular clusters are more of a mystery. Like the galactic hub, they are composed entirely of ancient "Population II" stars (*see page 36*). While all the globulars around the Milky Way are extremely old, astronomers have detected the formation of new globulars in the collisions between distant galaxies. Many astronomers theorize that our own galaxy's globular clusters are also remnants of such ancient collisions.

An X-ray map of the region around the galactic center, below, reveals several strong X-ray sources—each a stellar-mass black hole in its own right. The central black hole itself is in the middle of the image.

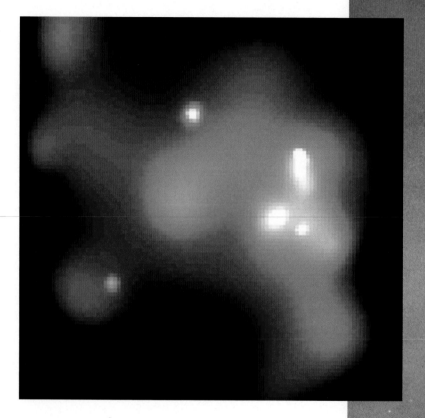

The central regions

The galaxy's central hub is roughly spherical, and approximately eight thousand light-years in diameter. Astronomers recently discovered that it is actually slightly elongated, stretched out along the direction of the Sun, and that the Milky Way may in fact be a "barred spiral."

Stars in the hub differ from those in the spiral arms. They include large numbers of old red and yellow stars that move in different elliptical orbits. They are also not tightly confined to the main plane of the galaxy. Hub stars are so different from the majority of the spiral arm stars that astronomers classify them as a completely separate type called "Population II" stars. Population II stars are the dominant stars in some other galaxies (*see page 40*). They also form dense globular clusters.

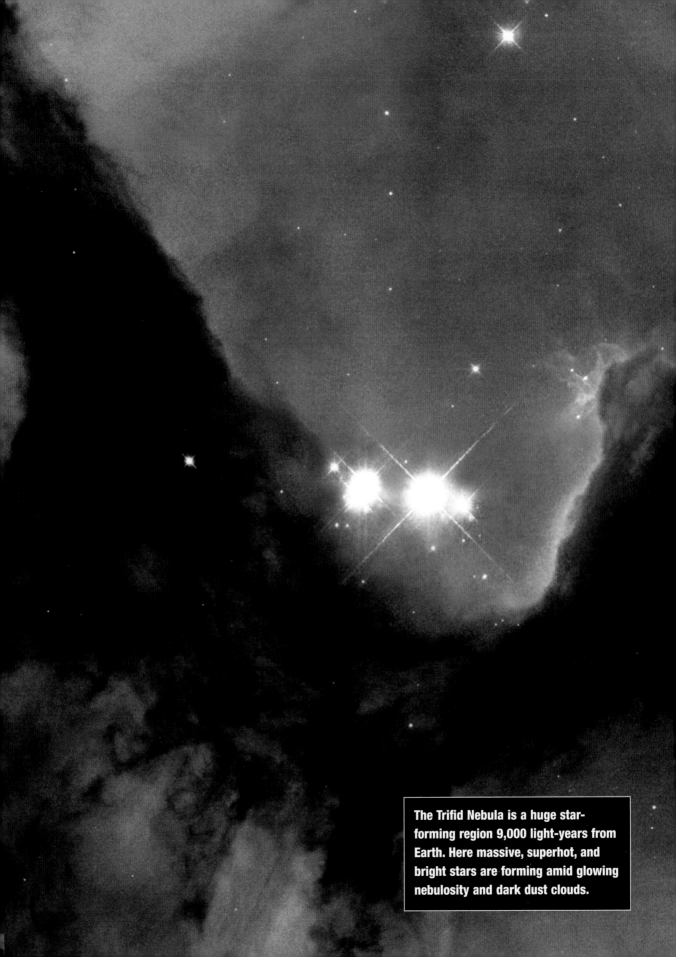

The Trifid Nebula is a huge star-forming region 9,000 light-years from Earth. Here massive, superhot, and bright stars are forming amid glowing nebulosity and dark dust clouds.

Why are the Population II stars so different? They live a long time and are abundant in the Milky Way's hub. Unlike the red and yellow dwarfs in the Sun's neighborhood of the Milky Way, Population II stars have a different composition, with lesser amounts of the heavier elements that help form the Population I stars. Astronomers believe these facts suggest that Population II stars formed long before the subsequent generations of planetary nebulae and supernovae had time to scatter the heavy elements throughout the universe. It's a good indication that Population II stars are very old. Their lack of heavy elements may also hold the secret to their longevity: Heavy elements increase the rate of nuclear fusion and shorten the life span of sunlike stars. So, although many other star generations have come and gone, the Population II stars still dominate the region.

Strange center

Although the galactic hub contains many long-lived and sedate stars, it is also an active place, littered with star-forming nebulae, bright young stars, and supernovae remnants. At the heart of it all sits the very center of the Milky Way. While invisible to light rays, radio telescopes can detect low-energy radiation from the area, and X-ray detectors and ultraviolet telescopes reveal extremely hot, energetic objects as well.

Apparently, an expanding ring of hydrogen gas clouds one thousand light-years across surrounds the Milky Way's center. Clusters of fiercely hot, massive stars within this hydrogen ring race around the center at speeds of up to 3 million miles (4.8 million km) per hour. The closer they get to the center, the faster these clusters move. They orbit a concentrated radio source called Sagittarius A*, which probably has an enormous mass of about 2.6 million Suns jammed into a space just a few light-hours across. Astronomers believe that only a huge black hole at the galaxy's center can explain this phenomenon. At present, our instruments are still too weak to confirm this.

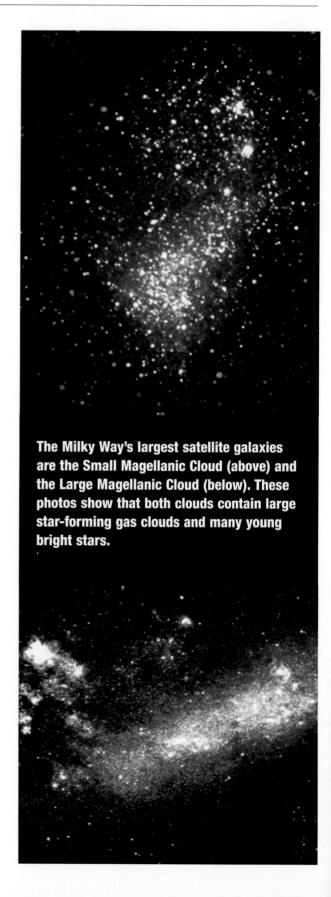

The Milky Way's largest satellite galaxies are the Small Magellanic Cloud (above) and the Large Magellanic Cloud (below). These photos show that both clouds contain large star-forming gas clouds and many young bright stars.

Galactic neighbors

The Milky Way is such a huge object that its influence extends far across intergalactic space. A number of smaller companion, or satellite, galaxies orbit the Milky Way. The largest and best known of these are the Small and Large Magellanic Clouds. These are clearly visible from the Southern Hemisphere as star clouds detached from the main band of the Milky Way. Other companion galaxies are smaller and fainter, as well as much closer to Earth.

The Magellanic Clouds get their name from Portuguese explorer Ferdinand Magellan (c. 1480–1521), whose report of them in 1521 was the first to reach European astronomers. (These star clouds were already well-known to various Native cultures.) The Large Magellanic Cloud (LMC) lies about 150,000 light-years away and roughly 30,000 light-years across. Its companion, the Small Magellanic Cloud (SMC), lies 180,000 light-years away and about 20,000 light-years across.

The most striking feature of the LMC is its abundance of gas, dust, and star-forming regions. One major emission nebula, the Tarantula Nebula, is so luminous that, if it took the place of the Great Orion Nebula (which is 1,500 light-years away in our own galaxy), its light would cast shadows on Earth. Even the parts of the LMC that do not show active star formation are still rich in young blue and white stars. The SMC has similar, but less spectacular, features.

The Magellanic Clouds orbit the Milky Way once every 1.5 billion years. These clouds are currently retreating from a close approach at which they came within 120,000 light-years of Earth. The Milky Way has torn away some of the stars and gases in both the LMC and the SMC. From our view (from the Southern Hemisphere), these trail along behind their respective main clouds as they continue following their orbit, forming the so-called "Magellanic Stream." Eventually, the clouds will be absorbed into our own galaxy.

On the other side of the Milky Way's hub, a faint star cloud called the Sagittarius Dwarf Elliptical (SagDEG), which was discovered in 1994, is crashing into our galaxy. SagDEG lies just 80,000 light-years away from Earth, but dust in our galactic hub blocks our view of it.

THE DISTANCE TO THE CLOUDS

The Magellanic Clouds played a key role in helping astronomers determine the scale of our universe. In 1912, U.S. astronomer Henrietta Leavitt (1868–1921) was studying a particular type of variable star called a Cepheid variable. She suspected that the pulsation period of these stars was linked to their true brightness. To prove it, she studied a number of Cepheids in the Small Magellanic Cloud (SMC). Since she knew they were very far away, Leavitt considered all of them to be the same distance from Earth. By doing so, their apparent magnitudes would be in proportion to their real brightnesses. Leavitt found that the brighter the Cepheid is, the longer its pulsation period. Ejnar Hertzsprung and Harlow Shapley used Leavitt's discovery to standardize, or "calibrate" (fit the information onto a scale) the data. The absolute magnitude of a Cepheid could then be determined from the pattern of its pulsations. This proved for the first time that the SMC was more than 100,000 light-years away.

CHAPTER 5

A UNIVERSE OF GALAXIES

There are at least as many galaxies in the universe as there are stars in our galaxy: two hundred billion or more. The sizes and shapes of these distant star systems—including gargantuan balls of stars or spirals like our own Milky Way, to countless tiny dwarf star clouds—vary widely from one extreme to the other. The enormous variety of different galaxies, their distribution across space, and the way that they interact with each other create great mysteries about the history of the universe and our place within it.

Classifying galaxies

Although each is unique, galaxies tend to form in just a few basic shapes. These include spirals (normal and barred), lenticulars, ellipticals, and irregulars. Edwin Hubble (1889–1953), the U.S. astronomer who first proved that galaxies lay far beyond the Milky Way, devised a system for classifying them.

The universe is packed with galaxies large and small, but we usually see only the larger and brighter ones that lie at great distances. Most of these are spirals and large ellipticals.

Spirals and barred spirals

Roughly one-quarter of all bright galaxies are spiral galaxies. While all are nearly the same size, the largest of these—such as our near neighbor, the Andromeda Galaxy—can get as big as twice the size of the Milky Way. Most spiral galaxies seem to have a supermassive black hole at the center of their hub.

Spiral arms in these galaxies show the brightest regions of star formation. The number, definition, and shape of the spiral arms varies. Hubble classified four different types of spiral, from Sa (with a large hub and tightly wrapped arms) to Sd (with a small hub and loose arms).

Barred spirals are similar to normal spirals, except that a "bar" of stars runs across the hub, with the spiral arms emerging from the ends of this bar. Barred spirals are classified as types SBa

The M101 galaxy displays its spectacular spiral structure beautifully.

to SBd. Another unusual variation is a flocculent spiral, such as the Triangulum Galaxy, our other nearby spiral neighbor. Such galaxies display a poorly defined spiral shape, with "clumps" of star formation instead of neat chains running along the arms. Both the barred and flocculent galactic forms may simply be phases that a galaxy passes through during its life span. Many astronomers theorize that these shapes result when a close encounter with the gravity from another galaxy disrupts the structure of a "grand design" spiral.

Ellipticals

Elliptical (ball-shaped) galaxies make up more than 60 percent of all galaxies. They vary in size much more than spirals, and include both the smallest galaxies (tiny and sparse dwarf ellipticals) and the largest (giant ellipticals, some of which may contain trillions of stars).

The stars in ellipticals are almost entirely old yellow and red "Population II" stars. These stars dominate because ellipticals do not contain enough of the gas and dust needed to form new stars. With no new stars forming, more long-lived ones survive alone as the shorter-lived, bright-blue stars die out. Each star orbits the center of the galaxy in an elliptical (stretched)

path. While stellar orbits in elliptical galaxies can tilt wildly, the lack of a distinct orbital "plane" and the fact that the stars are widely spaced keep them from crashing into one another. Without

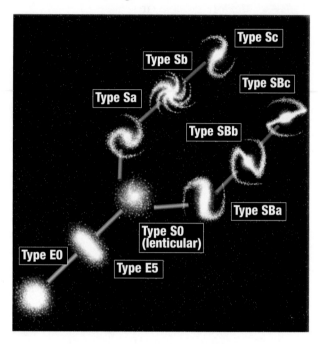

This diagram shows the method devised by Edwin Hubble for classifying different types of galaxies based on their shape.

Elliptical galaxies are dominated by longer-lived yellow and orange stars and contain very little gas or dust. They range from spheres to pronounced ovals, such as this one.

The Sombrero galaxy is a spiral with its edge facing Earth. Its dark "rim" is caused by dark clouds of gas and dust inside the spiral arms that block out some of its light.

gas and dust to complicate matters, their random motions are never flattened out into a disk. As in spiral galaxies, evidence indicates that most elliptical galaxies also contain a supermassive black hole at their center.

Ellipticals range in shape from perfect spheres to elongated ovals. In Hubble's classification, the perfect circles are E0 galaxies, and the most elongated ellipses are E7s.

Lenticulars

Halfway between spirals and ellipticals are the convex lenticular galaxies. ("Lenticular" means lens-shaped.) Lenticular galaxies have a hub of Population II stars surrounded by a disk of gas and dust but no spiral arms. Despite this, the disks contain a scattering of middle-aged stars. This suggests that, instead of forming from

Irregular galaxies are rich in gas, dust, and young stars. They are often sites of intense starbursts.

ellipticals that somehow collected a disk of gas and dust, lenticulars are probably spiral galaxies that lost their spiral arms. These differences may not be so great; lenticulars may also hold the key to the puzzle of galactic evolution.

INTERGALACTIC DISTANCES

There are no landmarks in space, so how do astronomers determine distances? In the 1920s, Edwin Hubble used Henrietta Leavitt's research of Cepheid variables to estimate intergalactic distances. He compared the spectra of Cepheids of known distances to spectra of more distant galaxies. Hubble discovered that the absorption lines of the spectra of the unmeasured galaxies were shifted toward the longer-wavelength, red end of the spectrum. This "redshift" became larger in the more-distant galaxies. Hubble suggested that the redshift was caused by galaxies moving away from Earth's vantage point in the universe. The expanding universe indicated by the redshift also correlated with the theory of the universe originating in a big bang. Astronomers now estimate the distance of a remote galaxy by analyzing the redshift of its spectrum.

These illustrations highlight only the hydrogen absorption lines in the spectrum of sunlight (top), and in the spectrum of a distant star receding from Earth (bottom). The absorption lines in the lower image appear shifted toward the red end of the spectrum when compared to the Sun's spectrum. The arrow shows the extent of the redshift in the spectrum of the distant star.

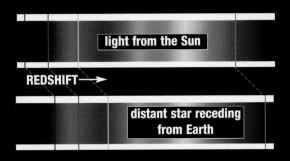

light from the Sun

REDSHIFT ➞

distant star receding from Earth

Irregulars

Irregular galaxies, such as the Magellanic Clouds on our cosmic doorstep, are rich in gas, dust, and young stars. This type of galaxy accounts for about 15 percent of all galaxies. They show little or no structure, but are often home to large star-forming regions. In some irregulars, called "starburst galaxies," the rate of star formation is so rapid that astronomers once thought these galaxies were exploding. M82, also called the "Cigar Galaxy," is the best-known starburst galaxy. It probably originated in a close encounter with a nearby spiral galaxy. Close encounters between galaxies themselves can initiate star formation in the same way that supernovae shockwaves and the gravity of passing stars can trigger star formation in our own galaxy —only on a much larger scale.

Clusters and superclusters

Galaxies like company. Although the distances between them are measured in hundreds of thousands, if not millions, of light-years, they are surprisingly crowded considering their size, and certainly much more closely packed together than most stars. Galaxies tend to gather in clusters and are held together by the gravitational attraction between them. Our Milky Way is part of a small galaxy cluster called the Local Group, It includes two other spiral galaxies, Andromeda (M31) and Triangulum (M33), as well as several dozen smaller irregular and elliptical galaxies.

The Local Group occupies a volume of space roughly five million light-years across, dominated by the gravity of the Milky Way and Andromeda spirals. (M33 is much lighter in weight and may actually be orbiting the Andromeda Galaxy.) The two major galaxies are themselves being pulled toward each other and will collide within a few billion years.

Galaxy clusters come in a variety of shapes and sizes. Our Local Group is insignificant in size compared to some. The nearest major cluster lies about fifty-five million light-years away in the direction of the constellation Virgo.

GEORGE ABELL

American astronomer George Abell (1927–1983) performed the first and most influential survey of galaxy clusters while working at the observatory on Mount Palomar, California, in the 1950s. He devised ways of identifying galaxy clusters among the randomly scattered "field" galaxies, and classified them into different types.

It occupies about the same volume of space as the Local Group, but is packed with spiral galaxies and large ellipticals, including several giant ellipticals at its center. Large elliptical galaxies are only found within crowded galaxy clusters, which gives us an important clue to their role in galactic evolution.

In 1995, the *HST* photographed Abell 2218, an even more impressive distant cluster than the Virgo Cluster. Abell contains more than two hundred and fifty mostly elliptical galaxies in a region just one million light-years across.

On an even larger scale, galaxy clusters blend together at their edges to form superclusters. These are the largest structures in the universe, often with a particularly large cluster at their center (the Local Group is part of the Virgo Supercluster). When astronomers mapped out the distribution of superclusters, they found that the superclusters formed chains and sheets around huge, apparently empty areas. This large-scale structure probably originated in the big bang, the enormous explosion that created the universe itself.

Active galaxies

Most galaxies shine with the combined light of the billions of stars within them. Others, however, are far brighter than they should be. Some show unpredictable variations in their radiation. Still more display features that are hard to explain. These unusual cases are collectively known as active galaxies, because their behavior cannot be accounted for through their star activity alone.

Active galaxies fall into four main types. Quasars and blazers are apparently starlike points of light that are actually very distant galaxies. The level of light they give off varies every few days. Some emit radio signals. Seyfert galaxies are similar to normal spirals, but have intensely bright central regions that are also variable. Radio galaxies are apparently insignificant galaxies, dwarfed by vast lobes of gas "glowing" at radio wavelengths. The origin of these lobes can often be traced back along jets that connect them to the core of the galaxy.

Although active galaxies show a wide range of different features, most astronomers now believe that the activity in these galaxies comes from the supermassive black holes at their centers. While the Milky Way's black hole is dormant, with no material close enough to feed it, the black hole in active galaxies is feeding voraciously. As it pulls gas, dust, and stars to their doom, the black hole shreds the material into an "accretion disk" surrounded by a doughnut-shaped dark cloud. The surface of the disk is heated up so much that it emits brilliant light and high-energy radiation. Some of the material pulled toward the black hole instead gets caught up in a powerful magnetic field, which spits it out at the speed of light and creates two jets of superheated matter at right angles to the accretion disk.

M51, the Whirlpool Galaxy (left), is involved in a close encounter with its neighbor, NGC 5195. Gravitational forces between the two have triggered great bursts of star formation in the smaller galaxy and have also turned M51 into a Seyfert galaxy with a bright, active core.

These gradually slow down and billow outward as they encounter intergalactic gases, creating huge clouds of glowing radio emission.

The type of active galaxy we see from Earth depends on the level of activity and the angle at which we see the central region. In radio galaxies, the core is edge-on—the doughnut-shaped gas cloud around it hides the bright disk, and the only sign of activity comes from the radio lobes. In quasars and Seyfert galaxies, we can see over the surrounding cloud onto the disk itself—the major difference between the two types of galaxy is purely the level of activity. In the rare blazers, we are looking "down the throat" of an active galaxy. One of the jets happens to point directly toward Earth, and this produces most of the electromagnetic radiation.

Active galaxies often seem to be involved in close encounters or collisions with other galaxies. Stars rarely collide with each other, but when they come close, they feel the pull of each other's gravity. The effects of this gravity often triggers spectacular starbursts. Direct collisions between gas clouds can heat the gas within a galaxy so much that it escapes the galaxy's gravity altogether in a process called "stripping." These collisions and close encounters can also send new material into the central black holes of galaxies.

Galaxy birth and evolution

Astronomers are still struggling to comprehend the origin and evolution of galaxies. The first galaxies probably formed in a similar way to stars, collapsing out of huge gas clouds. The latest theory is that galaxies formed around giant black holes left behind by an early first generation of supermassive stars.

Photographs from the *Hubble Space Telescope* that look far back in time show galaxies as they were shortly after the big bang. Many of these primitive galaxies are blue and irregular, with great starbursts occurring inside them. Often, the *HST* images catch them in the act of merging to form larger galaxies. This is also the era when quasars were at their most active. There is also a noticeable absence of giant elliptical galaxies in these early times. Astronomers use these clues to theorize how galaxies evolve.

As mentioned above, galaxies are very crowded together in space, and the gravitational attraction between them means that collisions take place on a regular basis. Collisions caused by gravitational forces may cause galaxies to change their shape. For example, collisions between spiral galaxies strip away star-forming gas clouds. By the time the colliding galaxies stabilize, the brighter stars have died. With no new generation to replace them, the merged galaxy becomes a ball of chaotically orbiting red and yellow stars—in

THE COSMIC TIME MACHINE

When we try to understand distant galaxies, we must remember that the universe acts like a giant time machine. Because light can travel no faster than 186,000 miles (300,000 km) per second, or one light-year per year, it takes time to cross astronomical distances. This means that we see things as they appeared when their light started out on its journey toward us. Within our galactic neighborhood, this does not really matter, but on the scale of the entire cosmos, it's important to realize that we are sometimes looking at galaxies as they were when the Universe was much younger. This is one reason that the most powerful active galaxies are more common at greater distances. We see such galaxies as they were when they were still in the process of formation, when more fuel was available to power their black holes.

other words, an elliptical galaxy. As more and more galaxies merge, giant ellipticals are created.

Of course, this isn't the whole story. Although gas from the spirals is heated and stripped away (clouds of gas are detected in X-ray pictures of old clusters), the big bang itself left behind some cooler background gas. Left undisturbed for a long enough time, an elliptical galaxy can collect a disk of this gas, turn into a lenticular galaxy with just a hub and disk, and then develop new spiral arms—the exact setting required for star formation to begin all over again.

Galaxy cluster Abell 2218 is so densely packed with galaxies that its gravity bends the light from more distant objects. Yellow galaxies are members of the cluster, while the blue-white streaks are warped images of galaxies beyond.

GLOSSARY

accretion: a collection of gases and dust in space caused by gravity; usually formed into a disk around a star that—because of its own gravity—collects more gases and dust.

aurora: striking display of "dancing" lights visible in the night sky near Earth's poles; caused by solar radiation interacting with Earth's upper atmosphere and magnetic field.

coalesce: to fuse or unite into a whole.

convection: the movement of heat through a gas or liquid; warm gases or liquids usually rise, then sink as they cool.

electromagnetic radiation: any of the various wavelengths of mostly invisible rays emitted by stars.

element: a substance that contains atoms of only a single kind. All matter is made up of elements.

flocculent: taking the form of a loose organization of particulate matter.

galaxy: a massive collection of stars and other celestial bodies held together by gravity.

infrared: invisible form of long-wavelength radiation given off by hot objects; also called heat radiation.

ionize: to cause an object to take on a positive or negative charge; ionizing radiation can change organic matter and cause damage or even death.

molecule: the smallest part of a substance, consisting of one atom or a group of atoms; has all the properties of the whole substance.

nucleus (pl. nuclei): the central, positively charged mass of an atom; accounts for nearly all of the mass of that atom.

photosphere: the visible surface of the Sun that generates intense visible radiation (light).

protrusion: an object that juts out from the surrounding surface.

radiation: usually invisible, and often damaging, energy in the form of waves or particles transmitted by stars and other matter, such as certain forms of the minerals uranium, thorium, and cesium.

satellite: an artificial or natural object orbiting a planet.

subatomic: relating to the inside of an atom or to particles smaller than atoms.

spectrum: an ordered arrangement. The colors in white light or the frequencies of electromagnetic radiation can be broken down so that the components they contain can be separated.

stellar: of or relating to stars.

ultraviolet (UV): damaging (ionizing), invisible electromagnetic radiation with wavelengths shorter than visible light but longer than X-rays.

X-rays: a form of invisible, ionizing radiation with very short wavelengths.

FURTHER INFORMATION

BOOKS

Asimov, Isaac. *The Birth of Our Universe; The Life and Death of Stars; The Milky Way and Other Galaxies.*
    21st Century Library of the Universe (series). Gareth Stevens (2005).
Couper, Heather, and Nigel Henbest. *Encyclopedia of Space.* Gardners Books (2003).
Graun, Ken. *Our Galaxy and the Universe.* Ken Press (2002).
Kerrod, Robin, and Giles Sparrow. *The Way the Universe Works.* Gardners Books (2002).
Miller, Ron. *Stars and Galaxies.* Worlds Beyond (series). Twenty-First Century Books (2005).
Sparrow, Giles (Ed.). *The Night Sky: Discovering the Universe from Alpha Centauri to Quasars.*
    Thunder Bay Press (2006).

WEB SITES

www.nasa.gov
Check out NASA's latest missions and activites.

www.space.com
Visit the best Web site for daily space news.

www.heavens-above.com
Track satellites and spacecraft and print out detailed star maps for your location.

http://antwrp.gsfc.nasa.gov/apod/astropix.html
View the astronomy picture of the day.

http://hubblesite.org/
Tour the wonders of space as seen by NASA's Hubble Space Telescope.

Publisher's note to educators and parents: Our editors have carefully reviewed these Web sites to ensure that they are suitable for children. Many Web sites change frequently, however, and we cannot guarantee that a site's future contents will continue to meet our high standards of quality and educational value. Be advised that children should be closely supervised whenever they access the Internet.

INDEX

Abell 2218 42, 45
Abell, George 42
absorption lines 41
accretion disks 43
active galaxies 43–44
Andromeda Galaxy 39, 42
Arecibo telescope 12
arrays 12

barred spiral galaxies 31, 34, 39–40
barycenters 11
Bessel, Friedrich 5–7
binary stars 25, 27
birth and evolution 23–24, 44–45
black holes 28
blazers 43, 44
blue giants 10
brightness 5–7, 23, 26–27

Cepheid variables 37, 41
classifying galaxies 39
clusters 33, 42–43
colors 8–9
convective zones 21
cool stars 8–9
coronas 15

density waves 32
differential rotations 19
disks 31–32
distances 5–7, 41

Earth orbit 6
Eddington, Arthur 23
electromagnetic spectrum 6, 12
elliptical galaxies 40–41
Eskimo Nebula 27

galactic neighbors 37
galaxies 39–45
gamma ray telescopes 12
gamma rays 6
globular clusters 33
granulation 17

Herschel, William 27
Hersprung, Ejnar 37
Hertsprung-Russell diagram 13, 15
hot stars 8–9
Hubble, Edwin 39, 41
Hubble Space Telescope 12, 45
hydrogen 15

intergalactical distances 41
IR (infrared) 6
IR telescopes 12
irregular galaxies 41, 42

Large Magellanic Cloud 37
Leavitt, Henrietta
    (*see also Cepheid variables*) 37, 41
lenticular galaxies 41
life spans 25–26
light-years 8
Little Ice Age 19
Local Group 42–43

M51 43
M82 42
M101 39
Magellanic Clouds 36, 37, 42
magnitudes 7
main sequence stars 12–13, 32
masses 8–9, 11
microwaves 6
Milky Way 31–37, 42
multiple stars 25

naming stars 33
nebulae 23–24, 26–27
neutron stars 28
New General Catalogue 33
novae 25
nuclear fusion 20, 23, 24–26

open clusters 33
Orion 5

parallax 5–7
parsecs 8
photosphere 15, 20
Population II stars 33, 34–36, 40
prominences 18
protons 20–21
protostellar clouds 23, 24
pulsars 27

quasars 43, 44

radar waves 6
radiative zones 20
radio galaxies 43, 44
radio waves 6, 36
red dwarfs 10
red giants 9–10, 26
redshifts 41

Sagittarius A* 36
Sagittarius Dwarf Elliptical 37
Seyfert galaxies 43, 44
Shapley, Harlow 37
Sirius 5, 8–9
sizes 8–9
Small Magellanic Cloud 36
solar cycle 18–19
solar flares 18
solar winds 15
Sombrero Galaxy 40
spectroscopy 20–21
speed of light 13, 44
spiral arms 31–32
spiral galaxies 31, 39–40
Spitzer Space Telescope 12
Sputnik 12
star birth 23–24
star types 9–13
stellar remnants 27–28
Sun 8–9, 15–21
    orbit 32
    position 31
sunlike stars 9
sunspots 16, 19
superclusters 42–43

supergiants 13
supernovae 28

telescopes 12
temperatures 8–9, 25
time machines 44
Trifid Nebula 34–35

UV telescopes 12
ultraviolet (UV) 6

variable stars 26–27, 37
Virgo 42
visible light 6

weighing stars 11
white dwarfs 10, 25, 26–27

X-ray telescopes 12
X-rays 6

DEMCO